# Soldiers of the Cross
# Book 1:

## *Rising From Perdition*
## John Evans

*Rising From Perdition.* Copyright © 2012 by John Evans

All rights reserved. No part of this book may be reproduced or transmitted in any form or by any means, electronic or mechanical, including photocopying and recording, or by any information storage and retrieval system, without permission in writing from the publisher.

ISBN: 978-0-9841386-5-4

Published by Chrysalis / Balm and Blade Publishing
1475 Hollow Road
Birchrunville, PA 19421
www.balmandblade.com

Cover art/design by April Silva (www.silvagraphs.com)

# ~ Dedication ~

I'm dedicating my first book to a friend that has been with me a long time. This friend has always been there for me and never lost faith in me, even though I sometimes seemed to lose faith in myself. She has helped me get through a lot and is still there for me. So I am honored to say that I'm dedicating this book to my dear and close friend, Elizabeth Brandenburg.

## Dedication

I'm dedicating my first book to a friend that has been without a long time. In life, we always have those for us and never lost faith in us and even though I sometimes seemed to lose faith in myself. Beth has helped me get through a lot and is still there for me. So I am honored to say that I'm dedicating this book to my dear and close friend, Elizabeth Brandenburg.

# Contents

*Introduction* ............................................................................ 1

Storming the Gates of Hell ................................................... 3
Red Storm ............................................................................... 4
Alone in the Darkness, Yet Not Abandoned ....................... 5
The Desert Pilgrim ................................................................. 7
Water Among the Flames ...................................................... 8
What a Simple Smile Can Do ................................................ 9
Rising From Perdition ......................................................... 10
Souls of Fire .......................................................................... 11
Grace Like Lightning ........................................................... 12
History on Flames ................................................................ 13
A Rose of Fire ....................................................................... 14
The Intensity of Sorrows ..................................................... 16
Messengers of Fire ............................................................... 17
Beams of Peace ..................................................................... 18
The Serpent's Last ................................................................ 19
Supernova: The End is Only Birth to a New Beginning .... 20
Baptism by Fire .................................................................... 22
Walls of Fire .......................................................................... 23
Trials Through Fire .............................................................. 24
The Last Explosion .............................................................. 25
A Tiny Spark Amongst Immense Darkness ...................... 26
The Book of Eternal Joy ...................................................... 27
The Cross and the Sword .................................................... 28
The Purifier ........................................................................... 30
The Forever Flame ............................................................... 31
Love that Burns .................................................................... 32
Rising From Perdition 2 ...................................................... 33
The Burning Bush ................................................................ 34
Fragments of Love ............................................................... 35

| | |
|---|---|
| The Road of Fire | 36 |
| Spark of Life | 37 |
| The Crimson Rose Opens at Twilight | 38 |
| The Martyr: In the Moment of Death or Eternal Flame | 40 |
| In the Heart of the Inferno | 41 |
| The Torch | 42 |
| Flames of Time | 43 |
| The Day of Passion: Love's Fiery Embrace | 44 |
| The Phoenix | 45 |
| The Thunder Rolls | 46 |
| The Cross of Flames | 48 |
| Fruit Tried by the Flames | 49 |
| Born of Flames | 50 |
| The Indestructible Dad | 51 |
| Arms of Warmth | 52 |
| Flying Among the Sunbeams of Life | 53 |
| Islands of Love | 54 |
| Chains of Perdition | 56 |
| The Darkness of Grief | 57 |
| All We Need is a Candle | 58 |
| The Soldier's Song | 59 |
| | |
| *Acknowledgments* | 61 |
| *Kickstarter Thanks* | 62 |
| *About Author* | 63 |

# Introduction

Fire is an unpredictable element. It does so many things on its own and seems to have a purpose to its actions. As humans, we admire it because we are seeking purpose in a world full of chaos and uncertainty.

Sometimes we try to avoid all the difficult questions and choices that need to be made. For years I was trying to figure out who I was and how to get out of the pit of darkness and grief I was in. I finally figured out that I can't do it on my own; it is impossible with our own strength. I don't care what anyone tells you: eventually you must face the fact that you need help.

I'm not some grand know-it-all; I'm just a teenager. I've made mistakes just like everyone else. But I choose what to believe in. And I choose to let the guidelines of my faith lead me rather than depending on some other human being who is just as faulty and corrupt as I am.

You have to be willing to love and lose. You must fight for your own beliefs. Don't conform to anything someone tells you without discovering it on your own first. Sometimes you may feel that you've come to a dead end, but the end is only the beginning. So enter the fire to find a new existence and meaning to life.

# Storming the Gates of Hell

Let us storm Hell's gates!
We are Christian soldiers,
Though sometimes we are scared to show it.
We must brave the fire and the flood
So we can bring others to the King and Champion,
Which is Christ our Lord.

3, 2, 1…
Falling off the ridges of reality and into the war zone.
Drop off!
We land right in the middle of Hell – the enemy's land,
Which is full of evil, but is driven back in our Lord's light.
Along with Christ, the Spirit is our Guide and fellow soldier.

So let us go through Hell in search of those to free from Satan's grip.
It is our duty as Christian soldiers to break the chains
And bring them to the Mercy Seat and God's grace.
The only weapon we have is the Word of God, our spiritual sword.
We also have the shield of Faith to stop the devil's fiery bullets.

So Christian soldiers, storm Hell's gates!
Go to the lost, proclaiming God's good news.
Never give up hope or peace.
Let Jesus guide you through the storm, fire, flood,
And even through the Gates of Hell itself.

## Red Storm

Red Storm is rising in the Heart.
It rises up at any time, uncontrollable
When you've felt wronged or cheated.

And the rage can cause you to do things
That you wouldn't do if you were thinking clearly.
It can cause you to hurt people both physically and emotionally.
Or worse: it can hurt someone spiritually
And lead them away from Christ.

Rage can also lead to revenge –
The spiritual disease that twists and destroys the soul.
We must ask the Lord to give us patience
So that we can control Red Storm.
If we don't, it will certainly take control of our lives.

Don't let Red Storm rise in your life.
Instead, let the Cross rise higher
And let your eyes be always focused there.

# Alone in the Darkness, Yet Not Abandoned

In our cold world, we often believe we are orphans in the darkness.
This is a lie, for Christ came and shed His own blood for us.

We are not alone in this dark world.
Christ came like a wandering stranger
With no responsibility to help us,
Yet He chose to save and rescue us
From our dark fate of eternal death.

So don't believe the lies of the devil:
You have no salvation
And you are doomed to this void world.

Instead, believe the truth and join our happy family.
Become an adopted son or daughter of our Savior Jesus Christ.
And remember: you are not alone.

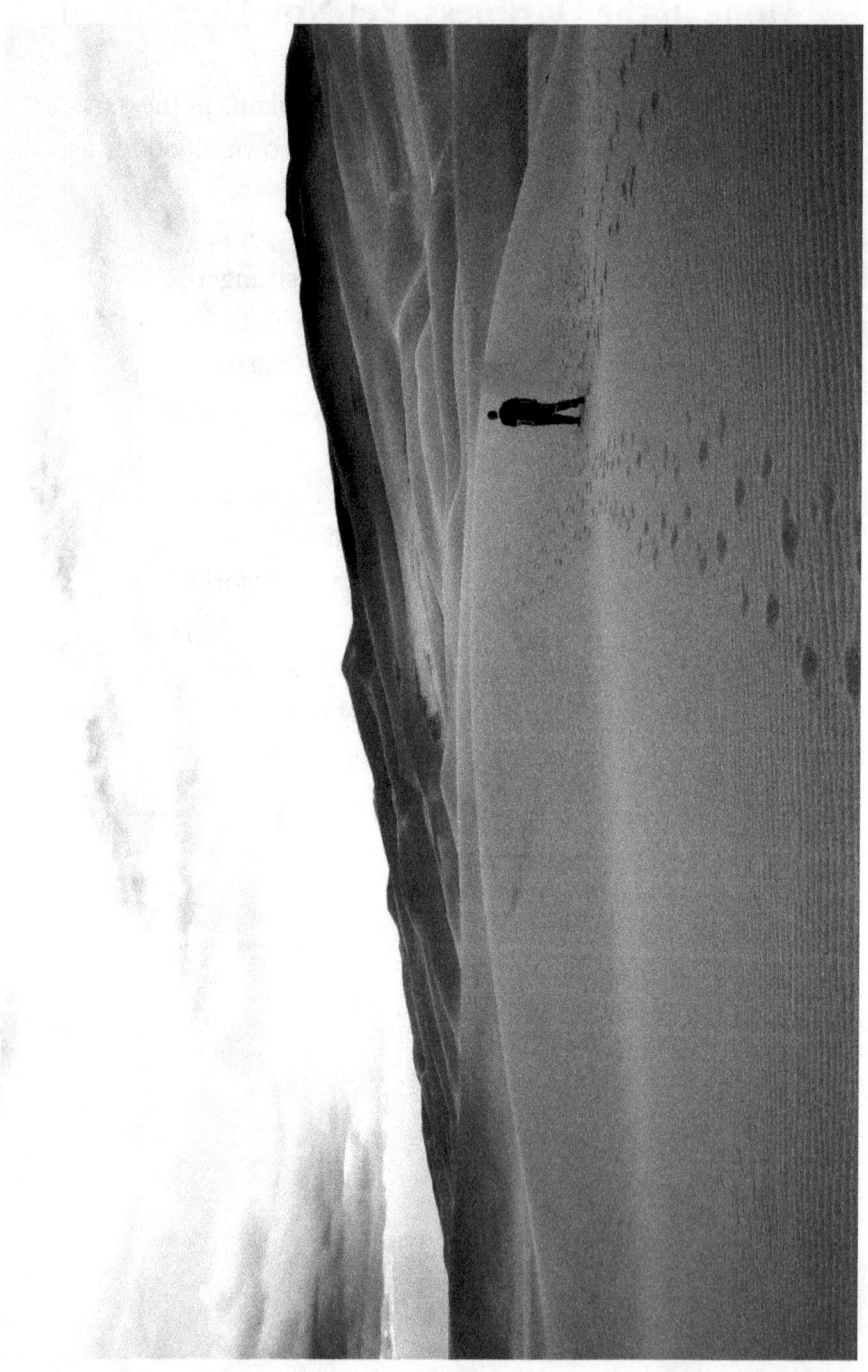

# The Desert Pilgrim

We are all Desert Pilgrims, wandering,
Looking for a country, a better land to go home to – our real home.
There are many challenges and threats ahead.
You'll be wandering almost all of your days.

But you have three basic things with you:
Sword, shotgun and water pouch.
Faith, the Bible, and the Spirit will be your traveling companions.

As a Christian Pilgrim,
Wandering through the sin-marred Earth,
Looking for the blessed, heavenly Promised Land,
We face many trials.

All of us will stumble
And most of us will eventually die
For a short period of time.
But if we place our faith and hope in Jesus,
We will receive eternal existence
When He brings us back to life.

Don't fear; have peace.
The Desert Pilgrim's journey goes on and on
But it will come to a triumphant end one day
When the battle of Armageddon is fought.

## Water Among the Flames

Natural flames burn everything they touch and nothing can survive.
Satan is like that fire, destroying everything he can.
We also destroy everything we don't like or don't understand.

God's holy people are sometimes scorched by the fire.
Yet we can also walk through the fire like water among the flames.
Even water can get burned and destroyed, and so can we.
Yet Christ has called us into the flames
So we can the save the lost souls it has snared in its fiery grasp.

So don't be afraid to cling to God
And He will be your shield and enshroudment of water.
When you brave this world of fiery demons and torrents of flames,
Put on the full armor of the Holy Spirit
And completely put your faith in the hands of our Jesus Christ,
Our heavenly Savior, who will help you be
Water among the flames.

## What a Simple Smile Can Do

A simple smile can turns a person's day completely around.
A smile can touch a person right to their very core.
A smile can turn a person from feeling dark and cold
To feeling warm and having a blazing fire inside.
A smile can lead a person to the greatest joy of all:
Our Lord Jesus Christ.

So never underestimate what a smile can do,
For it can hold great, untold power.

Unfortunately, a lot of things in this world
Steal the smiles from our faces.
The sad thing is that if people would smile at everything,
The world would be a much happier place.

So always remember
What a simple smile can do.

# Rising from Perdition

The world is on fire.
People live in the flames,
But they don't know they're dead.
The Earth is oblivious to its path of self-destruction.

Once, there came true salvation,
Pure water that the flames could not extinguish.
Yet the human race,
In all its evil and fiery hate,
Crucified Him on a tree.

But the princes of fire could not contain the water
That rose from the pit
Into everlasting life –
A spirit of pure water.

He calls us to come to Him,
To escape certain annihilation,
To cling to the symbol of the cross
As it rises out of the fire
With rings of water surrounding it.

All we have to do is jump
And embrace His everlasting mercy and love.

## Souls of Fire

We are all cold souls,
Brought into the world like still and motionless puddles of gasoline.
We can do nothing in our spiritual lives on our own.

It takes knowing God on a personal level
And letting His Spirit come in.
This ignites the gasoline, which makes our spirituality come to life.
Then we can truly become blazing Souls of Fire.

For as the old saying goes, it only takes a spark to get a fire going.
Our Souls of Fire can give life to other cold souls
With a small flame – that precious message
To point them to Jesus.

Souls of Fire,
Never let the Flame go out!

## Grace Like Lightning

How can I comprehend it?
When I discovered it,
It shocked me to my very core.
Christ's pure, relentless, self-sacrificing love
Was a new concept to me, a wanderer
In a word full of darkness and evil.

Even in this crooked generation,
God's love is striking everyone around us
Through our bright example.
God's sizzling, unrelenting love can be shared by us
And respected by others.
God's love and grace are free gifts from above,
Like the rain and lightning.

Grace has overcome the world and exploded,
Sending blessings to everyone who has heard.
How will you treat this electrifying grace?
Will you let it fly on by?

For as lightning flashes from east to the west,
God's lightning-like grace is going all around world
So that the world may experience the love of Christ' grace.

## History on Flames

They say history is written in stone,
That this world is destined to end
Not with a bang but with a whimper.

I say differently though.
I believe a simple and blameless man came to this world,
A world ruled by superstitions and falsity,
To shine a light in the darkness
And show us there was another ending:
One where, if we believe in Him, we could live on
And conquer death like He did.

The world did not understand Him
So it killed Him.
Death could not hold Him though, so He lives on,
And through Him and His Father
We can inherit the gift of eternal life.

So get some kerosene and take what man believes,
Take what the world and history books seem to point to: death,
Take it and throw it all into the fire pit.
Then light the match and throw the flame.
Light History on Fire.

## A Rose of Fire

What a simple thing a rose is!
Yet it has such an intricate design
And it can warm the soul.
It is also a reminder of a Creator
Deeply involved in His creation.

Yet it, too, will pass in the final days,
Like a blast of fire from the Creator,
Its true color and beauty will burst forth like a hot furnace
And will destroy those who destroyed the Earth.
The rose will burn up with everything else
When our planet is cleansed.

The rose can also give us a fiery, beautiful hope
That Lord will always be with us.
Yet we humans trample on it, ignorant to the truth.
Someday soon, however, those who admire it
Will trample over ashes in a world anew.

So remember Jesus through His creation,
His second book,
And the eventual fate of a Rose of Fire.

## The Intensity of Sorrows

My soul is tormented day and night
By what is and what could've been.
It seems I failed to help the people most important in my life.
The dragon continually burns and mocks me.

I could've helped so many
Yet I feel like I haven't helped anyone.
I feel like I deserve to be incinerated on the spot.
My soul anguishes for water yet I'm a dry desert inside.
Phantom guilt stabs my soul with rods of fire.
It taunts me with the fact that I'm nothing
And that's what I'm destined for.

Yet there's a part of me that will never die:
My loving spirit.
People may stab and kill me and tell me I'm naive
For being a forgiving and loving person,
And the sad, miserable thing is: I'm starting to believe it.

So I cry out to the Lord my Savior to quench my soul
For my sorrows have consumed me.
I feel as if my soul is nothing.
If I could I would give my soul away
So my brother could have the life he should've had.

My mind is a battle zone and I'm so confused about my worth.
I wonder if my own pains seem worthless in God's eyes.
It makes me feel like a man who is in extreme pain
And whose sorrows are like Jesus' sorrows.

## Messengers of Fire

Like cosmic radiation,
They go racing through the cosmos,
Delivering God's message of hope and rescue
To a war-torn planet.

Stationed on the planet are guardians
Who have been here through the countless ages.
These majestic beings have watched our planet for centuries
Yet have not been corrupted.

These beings of flames know the time is coming
When the conflict will close and God will take His people home.
A millennium will come and go and He will return
To make a final cleansing and purging of the earth
And the complete eradication of the dragon and his demons.

Then it will be like it was before the Great War:
Perfect peace in the cosmos.
The messengers won't be silent though.
They will still be carrying God's message of love to everyone.
They will still be God's Messengers of Fire.

## **Beams of Peace**

God's love never fails to warm a person to their very core.
There is one day a week when all the stresses of life
Seem to vanish from memory,
A brief twenty-four hours when all seems right with the world,
Where God's love fills and warms a tiny cold building
To the temperature of love.
There are beams of light from the sun that penetrate you
And give you the feeling of the utmost peace.
There is a cool breeze
That gives you the sense of freedom,
A certain tune that makes the heart weep for joy.
It all begins with God's Son, who brightens the world
And sends all throughout the earth
Beams of Peace.

## The Serpent's Last

Right before the end, even he shall acknowledge it:
God's ways are just.

This will have no effect, though, on this devil of old,
The Fiery Father of Lies.
He shall rally his forces for one last attempt to take the city,
But his army has lost faith in their commander.
They have finally realized what he has led them to.

Then God, in His infinite mercy and love, will finally end it
And put them out of their misery.
He will send out His eternal fire and burn them to ashes.

So finally that fiery dragon
Will experience a fire greater than him.
He will then breathe
The Serpent's Last.

## Supernova:
## The End is Only Birth to a New Beginning

Everything dies. We all have that unfortunate fate
Except for that perfect remnant of people.
We all have to accept this idea that we might die
Before Jesus' Second Coming.

Like when an overgrown forests burns down,
Yet out of the ashes comes new life.

The same is said for a star when it goes supernova.
Even though it explodes and creates a black hole,
It jettisons out new materials for other stars to be made from.

Likewise, we die in Christ and are buried,
But listen, here's the good stuff:
We will be raised into a new and grander life like He was.

So Christ's Second Coming will be
Just like a supernova giving birth to new stars,
Except we will be made into eternal beings –
People who are free from death.
We will join Christ in His likeness completely.
We'll then realize what it means
When the end is only birth to a new beginning.

# John Evans

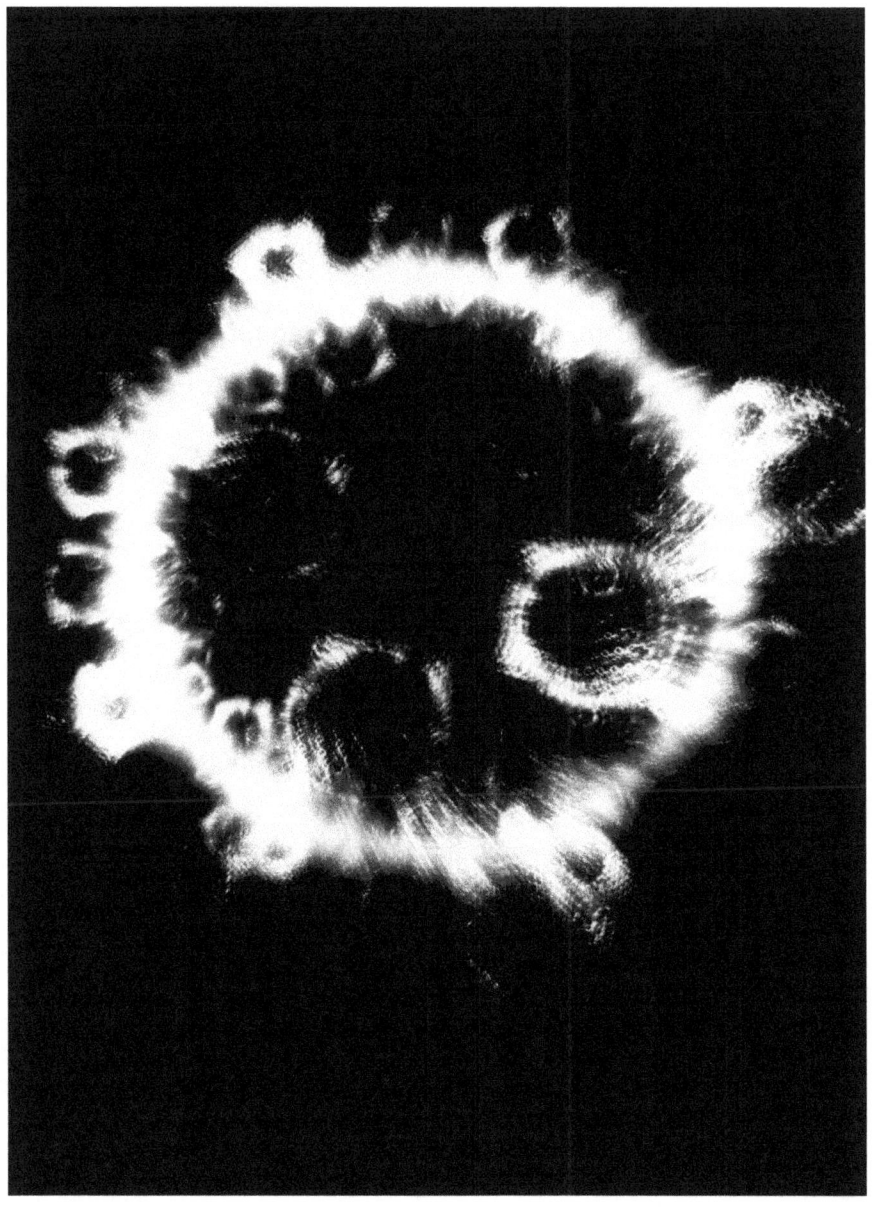

## Baptism by Fire

We are marching
Across the desolate wasteland called Earth.
Our Commander in Chief is Jesus Christ.
Our goal is to save as many souls from the enemy as possible.
Our enemy is indeed old: he is the father of lies,
Responsible for all the death on this once beautiful planet.

But our Father made the ultimate sacrifice for us
By sending His Son to die for us.
So now we march for His cause.
We battle with the enemy,
Wearing our spiritual armor
And wielding our Sword of Truth.
We beat back the tide of evil
Even though the devil's arrows and many pit traps
Push us and make us stumble.

We have an unbeatable commander on our side:
God's own Son Jesus Christ, who beat the devil and death,
So we march, knowing that even though the enemy
Will burn us and kill us,
These trials will make us stronger during Judgment day
And give us patience, which gives us endurance
To withstand our Baptism by Fire.

## Walls of Fire

Satan sets up many walls of fire in our world
To cause us to stumble and go down
And follow the wrong path towards our own destruction.

Against Christians, however, he throws a million walls of fire.
He hates us with a hatred that is not of this Earth.
He does this to burn and damage our souls,
To try to turn us against Christ.

We must, during these brief moments of persecution by the enemy,
Lean on the One who will surround us in the water of His love.
He will guide us through Satan's snares and walls of fire.

## Trials Through Fire

We face many trials and stages in life.
These can be hard if you don't know one thing for sure:
God's fiery, unending love will always be with you.

You need to remember this
Because we have an enemy, the devil,
Who is always seeking those he can corrupt and destroy.

Both he and God are waging wars against each other
For your very soul.
Ultimately the choice is yours.

That's why these trials are so fierce: because of you.
They aren't supposed to be easy.
After all, they are trials through fire.

# The Last Explosion

There comes a point
When everything must have an ending.
Everything has a beginning and an end,
God is called the Alpha and the Omega,
The Beginning and the End.

Yet we don't know if the saying is true.
The last human emotion
Expressed by those who love God
Will be a simple tear.

For the wicked won't end with a bang but with a whimper
When they truly realize the gravity of their choices.
For God's last great explosion on Earth
Will be that of a cleansing fire,
For the end is only birth to a new beginning
That will start with the strange act of God:
Out of mercy He will spark
The Last Explosion.

# A Tiny Spark Amongst Immense Darkness

Sometimes it seems in our dark world
That all hope is gone.
Put simply: this is not true.

Hope, when everything seems lost,
Will inspire us to love
And that love is Christ.

Just like Pandora's Box, even though evil was released,
Hope still managed to survive.
Jesus is hope and even though He was crucified,
He rose and gave man that tiny spark of hope
That today is growing at an incredible rate.

Even though it seems the world is getting more rotten each day,
We have this hope,
Because we know He's coming someday to take us home.
Jesus is in us and we are in the world as
A tiny spark amongst immense darkness.

# The Book of Eternal Joy

"What is Eternal Joy?"
You may ask.
Eternal Joy is a joy
That cannot be destroyed
By any means our enemies employ.

It is a joy that warms you
To your very core and can't be extinguished.
It's like a fire on a cool summer night or in a raging blizzard
Or the joy of a parent at the sight of their child
Being brought into this world.

It's a pure and endless joy
That starts here in the heart
And continues into eternity.

You may ask,
"Who gives this Eternal Joy
And how can I get it?"
You get it through the one Man
Who has conquered both the devil and death.
He is the Son of God and He holds Eternal Joy.

He is also willing to give it to anyone
Through His book, the Bible,
The book of Eternal Joy.

# The Cross and the Sword
(Based on Ephesians 6:10-20)

"Behold, our weapons for the war!"
The commander shouts.

In this battle of the heavenly realms,
We have God's Holy Shield of Faith
To stand against the dragon and his fiery roar.
And we have the Cross and the Sword –
Christ our Savior and the fiery, purifying guide of the Bible.

These forces aren't of flesh and blood.
They can't be destroyed by our devices of fire.
These forces are of the unseen world
And they battle for our very souls.

This is their ultimate goal:
Some to save us and others to destroy us.
So we must remember to put on all of God's Armor
And raise our coat of arms against the devil:
The Cross and the Sword.

# The Purifier

The Purifier.
This is one of the names of our precious Savior.

He finds us as moldy rocks,
Ultimately worth nothing at all
And deserving to be cast away.

Christ looks at us differently, though.
He sees what we could be,
So He purifies us in Fire
And molds us slowly
So we can become more like Him:
A stunning diamond of fire,
Shinning with Christ's righteousness and love,
Shinning in a world full of darkness and evil.

These tiny diamonds of fire
Illuminate Christ and beat back the darkness
To show His love to a people
Who are trying to purify themselves,
To show them that He is the only one
Who can be the Purifier.

# The Forever Flame

Most flames on earth burn out and die.
They don't last very long,
Like the lingering flame of a match:
Here for a moment and gone the next.

Flames are just like humans.
A spark gets us going.
We get warmer and warmer,
Then, half way through,
We slowly get colder and colder.
Eventually, we die.

This is the human fate we all have:
Destined to die like the flame.

There was one Man, though,
Whose flame was perfect and never died.
His name was Jesus Christ.
He died and was raised again for us
So He could give us the gift of the Forever Flames
That will never go out and will last for all eternity.

All we have to do is accept the gift and live in the Flames.
Then, someday, our mortal flames will turn into
The Forever Flame.

## Love that Burns

Some people believe love can burn you
Because of a bad experience.
I believe differently.
I believe there is a pure love,
A love that burns so strongly you are drawn to it,
Like a warm fire draws people in and opens up their hearts.
You are drawn to this fiery pure love.
Why?

You have never in your whole life felt this kind of love before.
Even though it blasts through the darkness
And reveals to you all of your faults and sins,
It also presents a Man who died and sacrificed everything for you.

This love will never abandon or forsake us.
It will lead you to a warmer and brighter life.
It is the only positive and good form of love that can exist:
Love that burns.

## Rising from Perdition 2

Ever since Eve ate the fiery red fruit,
Mankind has been in Perdition.
We do not know which way to go,
Who we are, or what our purpose is in the world.

All that changed though
When God's own Son allowed Himself,
In human form, to be nailed to a cross
By the demons and powers of this world.

All of the sudden:
Cleansing, purifying water was poured onto our world,
Beating back Perdition's flames.

All you have to do is believe in Jesus Christ
And cling to the Cross.
Then rings of water encompass the Cross and us.
The Cross changes us
As we rise higher and higher and
Rise from Perdition.

## The Burning Bush

How can we possibly explain a bush
That is on fire, yet it doesn't burn?
You can't.

In the same way, you can't explain
Destroying the soul with fire.
It isn't possible.

Like everything in this life, we have to take it on faith.
We believe that fire can keep us warm and possibly kill us.
We believe it from our own and others' experiences.
We believe in God, the Holy Spirit,
And His Son, Jesus Christ our Savior.

We believe because of evidence we see in Nature
And the written accounts we have of Him.
Yet when we start to see His influence
In our day to day lives,
That's when He really starts to become real to us,
And our Faith becomes real, not because we see Him,
But because we can see His actions on our behalf.

Just like sometimes you have to believe
That a bush is on fire
Yet it is not burning,
And God can be in that
Burning Bush.

# Fragments of Love

When a grenade explodes it sends out millions of fragments
Through the air, burning and tearing through the skin.

Fragments of love are nothing like that, though.
This is a pure and innocent death,
A selfless sacrifice.
This is God's grenade of love.

Dying for one's cause or for someone else
Really makes people think
About what you stood for and believed in.
In that way, your death is like a grenade of love:
It sends God's love out everywhere,
It pierces right through the person's body
And burns the person with conviction to their very soul.
It shows them compassion
And makes them more open to God's love.
So if you are afraid to die, don't be,
Because you will be giving one of the greatest gifts of God:
Fragments of Love.

## The Road of Fire

Everyone has perils in this life.
Stones had to withstand great fires
Before they had the strength to stand beneath our feet.
The plants had to withstand great winds
Before their roots had the strength to grip the soil.
Humans have to face many perils of our own.
We have to face the Road of Fire and trials of great challenge
Before we can truly figure out our calling in life.

Like the monks who train their feet
To withstand the fire and pain of the coals,
We must train our minds and soul
To withstand the temptations and things of this world
And the many deceptions the devil uses to hurt us.
He uses them any way he can
So he can ultimately pull us away from Christ
And seal our doom along with his own.

So let Christ mold you and form you
During one of the greatest times of peril in your life
On the Road of Fire.

## Spark of Life

What does it take to get life going?
A huge explosion or a supernova?
Was it some big bang as we humans call it?

No, the universe began with a command,
A voice that echoes through the ages with divine power –
A power that could create fiery light,
That could put the sun, stars and planets in their courses and orbits.
The divine being had the power to do all this,
To make all these things and other galaxies.

Life didn't begin by accident
But by God's intelligent design.
We were not born of fire,
But by the very hands of God.
He molded us out of the dirt of the Earth,
Creating our soul uniquely – there is no other like it.
We were born when the breath of God entered us,
When we received that Spark of Life.

# The Crimson Rose Opens at Twilight
(Dedicated to my dear friend and a constant person
who has been there for me in some seriously hard times: E.B.)

What do I say when you question why I love you?
I have so many reasons.
You changed me into a person I could never have been without you.
I would've been a loveless person without you.
You taught me that even though love is hard, it is worth the risk.

Love is crimson.
You have to shed some blood and work at it.
It takes time as well, and then it blossoms
At the precise moment of understanding
How much you really love this person.

Love can also feel like a stab in the back
When you realize, not that they screwed up,
But that you may have driven them away.
Love is timeless and will never forsake anyone.

Love came in the form of a girl who took me, shook me up a little,
Then brought me into an even closer walk with God
And unknowingly who He really is.
My life would've been completely different without that experience.

So cherish those you love.
Support those who care for you and love you deeply.
Remember that nothing lasts forever.
All we have are those certain moments,
Frozen in time and space,
When we dance and love among the flames
Like when the crimson rose opens at twilight.

## The Martyr:
## In the Moment of Death or Eternal Flame

The Martyr is one who sacrifices his life
For something he believes in with all his being.
What happens, though,
When this is a Martyr of Jesus Christ?
A Jesus freak?

We may be flayed alive or thrown into a volcano or blown up.
All these things are temporary moments of pain before death.
Then, after that, we have the blessing of waking up to eternal bliss.

The opposite is said for the wicked who persecuted us.
They will face fire and eternally die.
They face eternal fire and the Second Death,
From which there is no coming back.

So which will you be:
The Martyr or the murderer?

I will be the Martyr.
I will face a small moment of pain and suffering
Instead of dying truly forever
With no hope of ever coming back.

## In the Heart of the Inferno

There are storms in life.
Some are hurricanes or tornadoes,
And some are infernos.

When we are stuck in a storm,
What do we do?
We hide.

When you're in a hurricane,
What do you do?
You go to the eye of the storm,
For you know that's where it's safest,
And the storm is halfway over.

What's strange is that in life's inferno of sin and temptation,
We rush into the outer storm
Instead of seeking the eye, the light.
This alone is Jesus Christ our Savior.

So we get lost and hurt and trapped
In the darkness of it.
Instead, we should run full steam ahead with full
With confidence and assurance in Christ,
To the author and finisher of our faith.
We should embrace Him
As He constantly guides us
Through life, trials, temptation, sin
And even death itself.
For Jesus Christ is in
The heart of the Inferno.

# The Torch

A silent, single flame in the night
Giving light to a single person in the loneliness.

If this person has one light, this single little flame,
And is enshrouded in this never-ending darkness,
And is given a supply of oil that will never run dry,
Shouldn't he seek and help others light their torches?

This is the call we have as Christians.
We shouldn't hide our torches
Or let Satan blow them out.
We should go to others and show them
God's infinite love by our example.

In that way, we will be putting the oil on the torch.
It will then be up to God's Holy Spirit
To impress them to accept it as theirs and accept that hope.
In that way they will be lighting their torch and will have hope,
And there will be more lights shining in the darkness.

So always remember God's calling for you:
In this time of darkness,
To be a light-giving Torch.

## Flames of Time

There are few things that have remained
Steadfast and constant throughout time.

People aren't constant.
We all die and decompose.
Civilizations aren't constant.
They rise and fall.

One of the greatest constants,
And probably the most important,
Is Fire, which can exist anytime, anywhere.
You can keep it going under certain conditions forever.

Fire is a great spiritual symbol.
God spoke through it.
He uses it to cleanse and protect.

Flames are seen all throughout time.
It's a constant force used to destroy and inspire.
You can see it all over the stream of time.

One of the greatest things God will use it for
Will be to cleanse the Earth
And destroy the wicked, along with time itself –
Ending time and beginning the Eternity of Peace.

# The Day of Passion: Love's Fiery Embrace

The Day of Passion:
Loves Fiery Embrace.
This is not what you think, my friend.
I'm not talking about some mushy love between humans
NO!

What I'm talking about is the love that God has for you
And how he longs to embrace you in His ever-loving arms.
No mind can imagine, no soul can imagine
The things God has planned for those who love Him.
God's love is not like human love in any way.
He loves without reason and condition.
God's love is way out of this universe.
It has no bounds or restrictions.

Since sin came into the world,
Love even between two righteous people can die.
God's love never dies, for God is eternal.
Most important of all, someday God will take us home.

And on that
Day of Passion
We will experience
Love's Fiery Embrace.

## The Phoenix

Supposedly there was bird of either fire or ice.
Maybe even both.
It is legendary and mythical.
There is no proof that it is real and none that it isn't real.

The same is true with God.
We take it on Faith
That He is real and that He has a plan for our lives.
Yet many people, it seems,
Live life like it is a fire.
You're the fuel; you get thrown down
And you burn for a little while
And then you die and turn into ashes.

But there is a better way to live,
And that's in Jesus.
The best thing is that all you have to do
Is accept His gift and follow Him.

The only problem is if you don't
You really will be burnt up someday.
The plus side is that if you do accept,
Someday you will be able to stretch your wings of fire
And fly like the Phoenix.

## The Thunder Rolls

The thunder rolls.
The lightning cracks.
The world is shocked by God's righteous anger.
Do not ever think that God does not care.

When we lose loved ones due to disasters or calamities,
He weeps with the weeper
And is able to understand the sorrowful and grieved.
If He didn't, He wouldn't be a God of love.
If He didn't love, He wouldn't be God,
For the Scriptures say God is love.

So look unto the Lord in these times of uncertainty and trials.
He will comfort you in your time of need
And lead you through it.
Let God's love cover you and thunder out of you.
In all the things you do throughout your day,
Always remember God is a God of love.

So stand up. Don't be idle, but speak and act out.
Let you voice thunder about His grace and mercy
Just like in the rain and the storm.

## The Cross of Flames

The Cross of Flames.
Now I'm not talking about some KKK thing,
The people who go around burning crosses.
I'm talking about a cross made out of fire
That shines throughout all of eternity,
A fire that speaks to an evil heart
That's enmeshed in darkness,
A cross that was here from the very beginning.

The cross is a Man
Who was born through divine origins
And lived among us and chose to die for us,
A race that did not deserve to be saved.

Through this Man, this cross,
All are saved through His fiery, eternal love.
For when we think of our heavenly Savior
We think of the Cross of Flames.

## Fruit Tried by the Flames

Now tell me, who doesn't like
A good shish kabob?
You know what I mean,
Some fried fruit over an open fire.

Now imagine Gods' Holy Spirit's Fruit,
The ones we get by letting the Holy Spirit guide our lives
And transform our character.

You may ask how we can fry these fruits
Since they're your character and attributes.
With the purifying flames of Jesus.
When He purifies what current fruits are in us
And mixes onto the shish kabob His fruit
And only the best parts of our character,
Combined with His holy attributes,
Will emerge from the fire.
Plus, it makes them nice and hot to brand us
And convict us of the need to change.

So let your fruit be tried by God's fire
And let only the best come out of the process of
Fruit tried by the Flames.

## Born of Flames

We are born into this world kicking and screaming.
Since we were first conceived, our very nature was corrupt.
This was not always so though.

Our forefathers were not created
To kill, murder, and destroy,
Then perish in the flames.
That was the work of the devil,
Who deceived them
And diverted God's master plan.

The thing is, God knew what was going to happen.
He had a master Redemption plan.
So our Lord descended
From His holy, fiery realms of heaven
And He died for us on a tree.

So when we are baptized, just as He was,
We are actually baptized through fire into His death
And receive the privilege of entering Heaven's fiery realms
To live eternally with Jesus.

We will die in this world and be reborn.
In the next world, we will not be born of the flesh
But we will be born through Flames.

# The Indestructible Dad

He cares about us beyond imagination.
He would do anything for us.
So when the Devil came and kidnapped us
And stuck us in a hellish prison of fire and wickedness,
Did this Heavenly Father leave us to be abandoned?
No, He ran up to the devil's castle
And paid for our ransom through Jesus' sacred blood.
The devil said "Fooled you!"
Then God said, "You have no idea who you're messing with!"

He punches the devil's security device into oblivion.
The devil then launches his missiles of death at Him,
But God runs right at them and dodges and weaves through them.
They then come back and destroy the devil's walls.
God walks right on through after paving the way.
Satan launches his demons at Him, but God knocks them away.

God is seriously angry.
He wants His children back.
And He's not taking no for an answer.

Satan then takes off in his hellish ship
And God scales the building
And slings a grappling hook into the devil's hull.
He rushes across the rope and smashes through the ship,
Throws the devil into a wall like a toothpick,
He then proceeds to rescue His kids.
The last one is there and God says, "Jump!" He has faith and leaps.
God then destroys the devil and his hellish ship.
God and his kids then fly into eternity to spend it with
Their Indestructible Dad.

## Arms of Warmth

What do we do when darkness is all around
And the devil is about to devour us?

We go running into the arms of our heavenly Father
And ask for His divine mercy and grace.
We earnestly seek His forgiveness
And cling to Him with all our might.
Since God is a being of infinite mercy,
He will forgive you and wrap you up
In His eternal, loving, compassionate arms.
The devil will then flee from His presence
Like bats fly into caves to escape from the light.

God then guides us though the healing process,
For we so often beat ourselves up over past sins
That are like ash in the wind,
Forgotten by God who forgave us,
But not by ourselves yet.
For we still need to forgive ourselves
Before the healing can finish
As God wraps us up
In His Arms of Warmth.

# Flying Among the Sunbeams of Life

Life can be like a sunbeam:
Knowing your ultimate destination, yet
Uncertain how you are going to get there.

We began just like the sunbeam,
From a thing of immense power,
Except we are also from a being of immense love.

Just like sunbeams, we can be a thing of good or evil.
We can choose to bless people through our lives
Or destroy them.

Like the sunbeams, we can't exist on our own.
We draw our energy from God and His Son Jesus Christ.
In the same way the beams are made out of the sun,
We are made from God in His image and likeness.

So we can know someday we will be with Jesus.
We will soar from heaven
Flying among the Sunbeams of Life.

# Islands of Love

(Written in St. Lucia)

Past the mosquitoes, coconuts, and banana trees,
St. Lucia is a beautiful place, which you can hardly compare,
Though their faith was tested by the fire
(Technically speaking, a hurricane).

Through the blazing heat and the sweat of the brow,
I've grown very close to these unique people.
I've felt a special blessing while helping them
In their time of peril and its aftermath.
I've made special connections and bonds
That will last through this life.

So don't underestimate how resilient
We Christian brothers and sisters can be in times of trouble.
Also remember how we should run to help
And embrace each other in times of calamity.
Always remember, we are of one body and purpose,
One Island of believers in a sea of evil and chaos.

Christ sends us witnessing to a world in need of a Savior.
So let yourselves remember we are all star-crossed.
We are many Islands;
When one is in need, we should race to them
And comfort them, showing that we really are
Islands of Love.

## Chains of Perdition

What do we do when we're down in the gutter,
When Satan has you all chained up
In your own addictions and sins?

We ask God to forgive us:
Our sins against others
And all the stuff in-between,
Because we're human and aren't perfect.

We don't see the bigger picture.
We think that one prayer will overcome
A really strong addiction in one's life.
The plain truth is it can help a little but it can't overcome it.

The only sure way to get out of addiction's chains
Is to call upon the power of Jesus Christ.
Only then will you be able to break out
As you walk daily with Christ, accepting His help
To free you from the Chains of Perdition.

# The Darkness of Grief

In moments of intense sadness,
We often lose control of ourselves
And make the situation worse than it seems.

We let ourselves get consumed by the moment of the situation.
We let our memories of the past negative experiences depress us.
We lose the knowledge that God is willing to embrace us
And wrap us up with His love.

We forget that if we have sinned and repented for real,
Then we are forgiven.
Instead we let our shadow guilt consume us.
We lose sight of Jesus' offer of forgiveness.

If only we would embrace Him,
We would feel the fiery warmth of forgiveness
And mercy that only the Savior can give.
So all we need is to invite the Holy Spirit's fire into our lives
And daily surrender to Jesus and His warmth of love and joy
That will drive back the darkness of grief.

## All We Need is a Candle

All we need is a candle, the simplicity of a flame.
We want it to be the right kind of candle, though.
We want to be the kind
That goes out to share its flames with others.
We don't want to be the one that scorns and mocks
And turns what little sparks one has into damp coldness.

We want to look after our brothers who have tried
Time and time again to light their own candle
But couldn't do it.
It is up to us as followers of God
To be compassionate and help those in need.

There are also our sisters, who've been used,
And tried time and time again to do the right thing
Only to have it thrown in their faces.
God needs us to go to them and show them
That they matter and God cares about them deeply.
We can help them to light their candle.

So as we go through this world
All we really need to remember is this:
Does our candle have a flame on top?

# The Soldier's Song

So when he falls and his last breath has left him,
When he sees St. Peter, another soldier, he will say to him,
"Reporting, sir. I've served my time in hell."
Yet it disappears in an instant
And he wakes up groaning
For there is so much more for him to do.

In the same way, when we die in baptism to our old selves
Who didn't care about anyone but ourselves,
We are reborn and brought back to life.

For God can now do through us
Things He had planned long ago from the depths of eternity.
Yet more than ever Satan will try to destroy us
And ensure our permanent destruction with him.

So we can march proudly through this world now,
For Christ reigns and this war is almost over.
Christ is the victor,
So on resurrection morning, we can say,
"All here, reporting sir. We've served our time in hell."

This is the Soldier's Song:
To seek Christ with a reckless abandon
And to forfeit our own lives for His cause.

# Acknowledgments

I would like to thank everyone that has helped make this a book a reality, but there are a select few I would like to thank by name.

I very much appreciated the artistic abilities of Jeremy McIntyre, who helped me do my very first cover design. I would also like to especially thank April Silva, who helped me do the final cover design that you now see before you. Her abilities in digital art are very good and I would recommend her to anyone interested in having that kind of work done.

I would also like to thank two people who helped inspire me to write this book, delve deeper into poetry, and explore my own writing abilities: my English teacher, Mr. Greg Mosher, and my dear friend Jason Vanderlaan, who, through his own writing, inspired me to do what is before you.

I would also like to thank four more people who have always been like muses to me or challenged me to go beyond what I expected of myself. I am thankful for my Dad, step-mom, and mother, who have always driven me to do my very best. And I especially thank my dear friend Elizabeth, who I dedicated this book to, because she has constantly inspired me to keep pushing ahead even when I questioned why I should. She has inspired me to not only think deeper within myself, but has also helped expand the way I think. Most importantly, she represents what a true friend is.

The greatest person of all, though, is my Lord Jesus Christ, who is this book's true author. It is His hand that always guides my pen and without Him I would be totally lost and helpless.

From Your Friend and Brother in Christ,
Johnathan G. Evans

# Kickstarter Thanks

I would like to thank the following people for their generous contributions to our Kickstarter campaign: Garland (Granpa) and Norma Wyatt, Matthew and Beth-Anne White, Ted Vanderlaan, Matthew Lucio, Adelina Alexe, Elizabeth Brandenburg, Herb and Jeanette Shiroma, Trudy Shiroma Koeffler, David Koeffler, Mr. and Mrs. Elliott & family, and Rolanda Curtis.

## About Author

John Evans is a high school student at Indiana Academy in Cicero, IN. In addition to writing poetry, John enjoys running and working out in the gym. He also likes listening to music, traveling, and helping people. Even at such a young age, he is not afraid to face the difficult questions as he searches for purpose in life. He has discovered that the only way to survive the journey is to put his trust in a God who loves him.

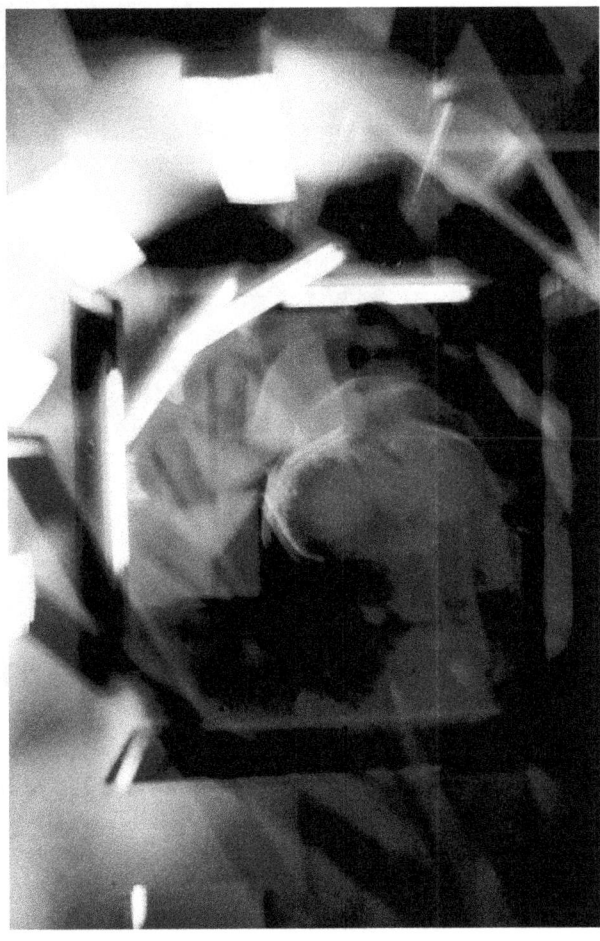

# What is Chrysalis?

Chrysalis is a new division of Balm and Blade Publishing. It features authors who show a commitment to using creativity to convey their ideas about the holistic human experience. Chrysalis especially focuses on mentoring new and young authors, helping them get their work out there even as they grow and develop as writers.

For more information, please visit: balmandblade.com/chrysalis

For the latest news and updates
from Balm and Blade Publishing,

please visit our website:
balmandblade.com

or join us on Facebook:
facebook.com/balmandblade

# Also available from Balm and Blade Publishing

Daniel de Sevén takes us on a journey deeper into doubt through a variety of creative essays meant to recall dormant doubts in the reader or else to create new ones. For many it will be an uncomfortable adventure but it is, the author argues, a necessary one because doubt is the delivery room of faith.

But be warned: this book isn't about the author trying to inductively prove a point. Rather, it is at once disjointed and communal, allowing readers to join the discussion and reach their own conclusions.

T. Jason Vanderlaan is the author of *Unspoken Confessions,* a book that wrestles with the issues of sexual addiction, lust, dating (especially how men treat women), and purity. More than that, it is an attempt at honesty – we all struggle with flaws of our own and with receiving the grace of God.

*Unspoken Confessions* is a call to find light in the darkness and to allow God to create a new heart in us as we seek to develop healthy relationships.